CANTOS TO BLOOD & HONEY

This book was funded in part by a grant from the Eric
Mathieu King Fund of The Academy of American Poets.

Cantos to Blood & Honey

POEMS BY ADRIAN CASTRO

COFFEE HOUSE PRESS ☕ MINNEAPOLIS

ACKNOWLEDGMENTS: The author thanks the editors of the fol-
lowing magazines where many of these poems first appeared:
*Bombay Gin, New Censorship, Make Room for Dada, Exit Zero, Paper
Dance: 55 Latino Poets (Persea Books), Conjunctions, Little Havana Blues
(Arté Público Press), A Century of Cuban Writers in Florida (Pineapple
Press), Long Shot, TRIBES, An Ear to the Ground (Cune Press), Poetry on
Stage (Poho Press), Forkroads,* and *Bilingual Press Review.*

Coffee House Press is supported in part by a grant provided by
the Minnesota State Arts Board, through an appropriation by the
Minnesota State Legislature, and in part by a grant from the
National Endowment for the Arts; The McKnight Foundation;
Lannan Foundation; Jerome Foundation; Target Stores, Dayton's,
and Mervyn's by the Dayton Hudson Foundation; General Mills
Foundation; St. Paul Companies; Butler Family Foundation;
Honeywell Foundation; Star Tribune/Cowles Media Company;
James R. Thorpe Foundation; Dain Bosworth Foundation;
Pentair, Inc.; Beverly J. and John A. Rollwagen Fund of the
Minneapolis Foundation; and many individual donors. To you and
our many readers across the country, we send our thanks for your
continuing support.

Coffee House Press books are available to the trade through our
primary distributor, Consortium Book Sales & Distribution,
1045 Westgate Drive, Saint Paul, MN 55114. For personal
orders, catalogs, or other information, write to: Coffee House
Press, 27 North 4th Street, Suite 400, Minneapolis, MN 55401.

LIBRARY OF CONGRESS CIP DATA
Castro, Adrian, 1967-
     Cantos to blood & honey / by Adrian Castro.
          p.   cm.
     I.   Title.
PR9205.9.C37C36   1997
811--dc21   97-16016
                                                       CIP

10 9 8 7 6 5 4 3 2 1

Para Mario y Pura,
fertility gods to my biology

———————————— ∂⟲ ————————————

Gratitude and praises to the following for support & inspiration: Jessica Roseman, Glenn Edwards Gant (Sharkmeat), Jeffery Knapp, Bob Gregory, Robert Antoni, Virgil Suarez, Jose Bedia, Rene Ramirez, Ramona Salazar, Edouard Duval-Carrié, Jerry Gonzalez & the Fort Apache Band, Mitchell Kaplan, and of course, Victor Hernández Cruz, friend and silent mentor of these lines. Adupe Olodumare, Oshun, Ogun, Elegba, Orunmila. Tó iban Eshu.

Blood is liquid life and honey is the flavor of it—El sabor. This is the Caribbean opened up, the details of the interior. These poems are a Caribbean projection realized—this is not merely a search for Antillean history and identity. Adrian Castro has sipped right out of the pulp and texture of it, has bounced right out of a drum beat with a caravan of words to guide us back to these tropical sensations which have fermented in the center of his memorial islands and sing in the diaspora of his humid imagination. No doubt he has heard the messages of Cuba's Nicolas Guillen and Puerto Rico's Luis Pales Matos; he knows also the breezes and the movements of North American poetics. He makes all these hermit and popular ingredients dance with each other. He brings us a manifestation in a fertile English crisscrossed with Spanish and African/Arowak vocabulations that have survived in the Caribbean and invented permutations of their sounds and sense. Life sparkles through this linguistic energy, a voice that encompasses so many tribal explosions. This is the history of syntheses, of what has come together: Andalusian/Mediterranean olive oil, the native people whose energy, foods, and cigars have not disappeared, the African who sprang away from slavery. All have survived, evolved, and have created a kaleidoscopic noble culture. In the Caribbean, drums have been made out of steel oil containers, out of wooden barrels that once contained bacalao, hand drums out of circular wooden cheddar cheese containers. It is a theater of improvisation and experimentation put into action by the need to overcome some of the harshest systems of exploitation that the earth could offer. These words are elastic with hope, they are prescriptions for healing, through a cadence full of pinpointed knowledge. Reading these poems is like ritual itself, like ceremony. Castro's criollo tripolarity and polyrhythmic versing approximate chant. The poems are clear maps of migrations, from the indigenous Orinoco and island hopping, to the Spanish sailors who vanished into Siboney maracas. The sounds of the Yorubas upon wooden vessels crossing the Atlantic, singing the first salsa into the stars. History is organized burglary. Adrian Castro has realized his geophysical position in the spider web of Caribbean history as an individual and as a larger portion of blue space. Reading these poems is like spinning within a mandala spiraling through personal observation and historical intuition.

If Chano Pozo the Cuban drummer who conspired with Dizzy Gillespie were hitting the keys of a typewriter instead of the skin of a drum, this is what he would have written, for the poetic meters contained in this book are based on the beats of a timba (conga), and they pulse to dance out of your hands.

Welcome, Adrian Castro, a Latin Jazz musician of Language.

—Victor Hernández Cruz
Puerto Rico

Contents

Herald of Cocos

The First Beats ... Ki-Lak

IN THE BEGINNING (I)

There were wails echoing
from riverbanks
mining for gold
fertility hidden in shells & stones
cascades made everyone
quietly deaf
In the beginning there were chains
entwined on legs like serpents on sugar cane
the bleeding syrup made the steel stick
many horses were bitten with machetes
There were processions of scars & piercings
tattoos talkin' 'bout tribe y history
bits of flesh flew from whips
& landed on island soil
(giving birth to a new people)

Crio-o-o-o-o-ollo!
Those with one foot chiseled in the islands
the other strutting Yoruba, Arará,
Kongo, Carabalí—
daughters of Oshun
sons of Hebioso
Ganga Nsasi owning aunts & uncles
brave men of Ekué Abasí

They gathered among the breeze
& pitched projectiles of words
into the shade
talkin' 'bout tribe y history

who they be where
they come from
Ifé, Guinea, Oyo, Dahomey,
Takua, Iyesha
They gathered among the breeze
in tribal organizations
that is
cabildos
the wise the ancestral were remembered
gourds of memory spilled
to refresh the present quench
the future
Tales of animals & flora going through shit
delivering messages that
everything is alive
todo tiene ashé
el café la guayaba el pan las hierbas
branches invading the sky
Un coco hovering above
waiting to crack open &
say something deep

You see
there were no books around
& what would a victim do with the murder weapon
anyway—
memory was survival
Tales in song in dance in music
Tales of little clay men & women zombied
bereft of language
Tales of the first African albino
endowing sculptures with echo

(evidence of life)
of lizards spreading wisdom in the four directions
with their pivoting eyes
tales of much thereof
within the backdrop of imagination . . .

The wedding between Spain & Africa
happened long before
the time had come for deities
to be sculptured & given vows to bow
before wooden crosses
Dios God Olofin
Olofin & Dios God
Saint Barbara y Shangó
Shangó & Santa Barbara
La Caridad Del Cobre & Oshun
Oshun y La Caridad
Our Lady of Mercy Mercedes y Obatalá
Obatalá & Las Mercedes
San Francisco of Assisi y Orula/Ifa
Ifa & San Francisco
Our Virgin of Regla y Yemayá
Yemayá & La Virgen de Regal
Ceramic faces were often even
black
though often even
cracked
when a drum spoke
gun-ki-lak gun
ka-ki-li-ki-lak
ka-ki-li-ki-lak
gun-ki-lak gun

They gathered among the breeze
talkin' 'bout tribe y history
eyes bloodshot & purple lips
though often even with drums
spilling gourds of memory
sealing their survival
Un coco tumbled & split
into four pieces
everything was OK
their pulp pointed skyward
todo está bien
the story continues . . .

DECEMBER 31, 1991

Este scent de gardenia
brings into my tanned hands
forgotten history

We bless every door
every window
with the ether of jasmine
the smoke of basil/albahaca
A candle lit for Eleguá wá wá
messenger & keeper of all doors
to shoo evil spirits
mal de ojo
that may seep into the ham hocks
brewing in red beans
that may prevent yr arrival
at the gate to the land where
quetzal feathers are skin & no one
has forgotten their history or
los cuentos de negros
de indios
de Andalucia

Este scent de gardenia—
it is the eve of another new year
where some will celebrate
the 500th year of a
wandering Jew
un marrano
bumping into paradise

others will mourn the genocide
of their genes
& yet others will sail
on yachts made from ceiba trees
across the Atlantic
to discover Europe

There is an infantry of serpents
circling
stealing feathers from quetzal
We are not dead
this culture & rhythm no se ha
has not melted
From Carlos Fuentes—
the Old World is now the new
the New World the old—
From José Vasconcelos declaring
      RAZA CÓSMICA
a trinity of colors blended as one
The stolen feathers are flying
East

Este scent de gardenia
brings a memory of fire—
of the humidity of jungles
where I swung on hammocks
hung clothing on palmas
drank café
waiting for the day Trujillo would fall
waiting for the day the land Betances & Hostos
promised
waiting for the day Batista would die—

of the night I gave my Dominican love
a gardenia hidden from Casanova's garden
just prior
to making love on a beach in Puerto Plata
on which we later danced
on a beach in Puerto Plata
on which marines then landed—
of the night Martí read his odes
& I was the echo for his words—
of the relentless tongue of Haitian sun
licking the spot where L'Ouverture
regardless of red black or white
saw that every bird
though asleep
has the potential to fly—
of the entire year I spent
blowing out the fires
Antonio de Osorio
governor of Santo Domingo
set in the name of Christ
conversion
España/Spain
the entire island in pain
a burning tabaco
a pit of volcano—
of the night I kept the candle lit
his pen wet
so Bartolomé de las Casas
could declare that 10 million Indians
were being massacred—
of the guayaba cassava
mango & chicha

I shared with a Taino chief
on the eve I became his scout
Agueynaba—
of the night I hijacked
on the edge where the Atlantic & Caribbean kiss
a boat full of Yoruba slaves
& returned them personally
to the palace of Shangó—
of the meeting between me
& my father
un negrito bembón
priest in a religion
their language spoken with drums
batá

Este scent de gardenia
brings into my tanned hands
on the eve of another new year
a memory of fire
a history that was altered
by lying tongues
a history that will change
beginning mañana

Cuba Santo Domingo y Puerto Rico
the trinity of rhythm
y sabor

EVERYTHING IS ALIVE

What wise feet embraced by buckskin
tread this land inviting
sacred objects:
bits of coconut to divine the future
incense y tabaco to quiet
bloodless eyes gawking at yr shadow
corn for a tricky destiny
cotton to dress peace when it arrives
a silver rooster announcing
wisdom's footsteps
Sacred object aboriginal style
in sacred spaces
Everything is alive

Alive was the neon of idols
killed in action
overwhelmed by the old rhythms
of sacred spaces:
altars of electric candle where they sprouted
carrying a Taino chief
in their shadow
hunting the misplaced city
of immortality
Glass   steel   concrete bent
like a Dizzy Gillespie trumpet
striving to reach a stale god
They lived among a breed
with Styrofoam hearts
who gathered short attention span books
then used for confetti who

gathered cars   planes   trains   hid
paintings with images that migrated

Clocks were a summons for history
history an offering for memory
Sacred object conquistador style
in sacred spaces

Everything was dead
But everything is alive

POEM TO GREET YOUR MEMORY

The face that is celebrated
is the face that is shed
after the last sigh
Not any face in particular
but that one
the one that inherited a nose
perhaps a blinking pattern
from the past or
thick ankles
not any in particular
perhaps some that strolled a different earth
the one remembered in a dance of masks

Around a sandy lake they wear
other people's clothing
Men have beards & large teeth
Women
paint their eyes in wave patterns
& this
may fool several spectators
The wavy eyes ask
if everyone is certain of what they see
Is everyone certain of what you see

There were ducks performing drunken struts
The one vested in white plumage
reminded us
dijo el pato in kuekueyé language
we are of tropical blood

no matter how you paint yr face
you
will always be del Caribe & her waters
you
were born in a downpour
of heat & humidity

We sat on the rim of that lake
waves would keep paddling messages
with those brass oars
the waters would not calm for a while
for there were enough people
to fill a calabash-sh-sh
A turtle was arguing with several alligators
many a witness said it got heavy
something like
no animal should kill its own kind
for we've the same ancestors
something like
how origins tend to curl like a wave
then break
curl like a wave
then break
curl then break
bits of ancestors clotting each froth

Entonces/then
then/entonces
yes we can resist the urge to forget
(se puede)
yes we can glimpse into each bubble
we can aspire to greet those three masks

(se puede se puede)
yes we can speak their names
the past the present
imagination
the wave in her eyes
the shell for the turtle
the needle that guides the thread
Punto y aparte

POEM TO GREET YOUR MEMORY (II)

What dishes would burst if you
were never mentioned again
Days are huddled in cities while
dressed in rainbow-colored robes
But no one recognizes the scars of honey on yr
cheek
There aren't any elders who nod
who say I remember yr birth
yr initiations yr marriage yr children
even the dancers at yr funeral
And you still look the same
I recognize you
You hoped the elder mulatto with
bone guayabera had said something
like this
But no one stares at the dated ragged clothing
at the historical events on yr brow
at yr habit of spilling café on the floor
You have arrived at the city where the mayor
cannot recall his name
& relishes this idea

So you walk the city for a week
with a little magnet in yr pocket—
this is to attract the strength of memory
This was the amulet so everyone would remember
This was how you did it before

The festival of borrowed cloth that summoned
women with waves on their eyes

men with large teeth
This was done to get their attention
to make their histories
curl like a wave
then break
make sure they were certain
of what they saw
Are you certain of what you see?

Perhaps you inherited a nose
a unique blinking pattern
thick ankles
(this is no doubt
because you once walked too much)
Yet no one recognizes the festival
& the one prior
on the shore of that lake
the messages her waves paddled
on a brass boat
towards the rim
of a calabash-sh-sh

Blup-blup-blup the cauldron
blup-blup giggles blup
Doña Ramona summons the paprika spirits
What has happened to the santos of salt 'n pepper
while crossing the Florida Straits?
The ululating swoosh-fffwwha undulated whisper
the Caribbean Sea so thick you cd put it in your pocket
I once recalled a past life where I
drowned floating on a big black rubber doughnut
fleeing the buildings los yánquis built
knowing they'd hit water eight feet towards hell
teetering on lodo
on muddy foundation

℘

Water
everywhere you look water
water on yr hammock
water in yr wallet
yr self-determination watered
y mas agua in the clouds stenciled after Cuba
after Santo Domingo
after Puerto Rico
Ando don't forget those mango trees
guayaba trees
that is
mambo
that is

rumba trees
those son montuno trees

~

So what happened to the shoeshine boy
who cracked the rag real quick whip on wing tip shoes?
Fuck wing tips
We're in el barrio now
& many here tread in borrowed shoes!

A baby with diapers bien sucio
screaming da-da!
Screaming huy mamá que está caliente!
Screaming gimme some arroz con gandules some quimbombó!
Screaming those hormones keep taking target practice!
Screaming soy inocente bail me out of jail!
Screaming I'm not the father!
Screaming I'm yr equal!
Screaming to his father you are not my equal!
Screaming at walls to hear the echo of his own voice
to find his original rhythm
the pssh-tah pssh-tah clink clank clunk of his own body!
Screaming I got these bruises on my hands my back
& I forgot how they landed there!
Screaming I've lost my teeth in a bowl of kalalú!
Screaming I have fifty-four grandchildren y nadie me
      viene a ver!
And on that epitaph: I wrote a poem once
turned out to be my story

All these colonies
tanta gente santa—
pieces of the Caribbean
teeming in New York San Francisco
Los Angeles in Miami—
wrinkled faces sucking from a mountain's breast
silver-headed folks pulling sixty hours in la factoría
to pay for pawned hope
The hope that tells them
self-reliance will one day
algun día be more obtainable than food stamps
And they pray to papa Dios to Babalú Aiyé
y todos los santos
offer them a glass of water some pennies
una manzana or other fruit
y un tabaco
so their children & their children's children
won't have to work the same job
be something they like
be a healer a doctor an engineer
a teacher even a poet
so they can
one day while looking at a winking graveyard boast
"Mi hija es una doctora
my son is an engineer
mi otro hijo es un poeta"
The mountain's breast has watery milk
La factoría will become obsolete

✌

Though we stand on a street corner
we wait powerlessly for the person
perhaps Gregorio's mother Doña Casandra
who talks real fast & real loud
to announce that Spanglish
is the official language of this barrio
we walk from bodega to bodega
from botanica to botanica
looking for the ingredients that will shape the stones
the stones that were brought from las Antillas
las Antillas that have shaped our skin

~~

We scroll backwards in history
From this town
far from el aguacate
from televised dreams of humidity
far from the winds
that kill people from flying mangos
to mambo kings blowin' baby blowin'
sweaty mojo charangas in Calle Ocho—
to when Desi Arnaz didn't speak English—
to when Puerto Rico lost its independence—
goin' back to when France owned Santo Domingo &
Haiti
way back to when Bartolomé de las Casas
declared slavery evil while swinging on monastic ham-
mocks—
goin' way way back to when
lusters of gold dancing hypnotically in Caribbean rivers
spoke in tongues

when palm trees summoned lightning
whom you asked when lost & wandering
whether one's treasures were going to be found
Columbus never found those treasures
those treasures were always there

❧

Blup-blup-blup the cauldron stuffed with frijoles
blup-blup keeps giggling blup
No one knows what ever happened to Doña
Ramona—
she might've gone swimming in the olive oil
she might've sailed back on the Florida Straits
she might've blended
with the salt 'n pepper

THE LOGIC OF GOATSKIN

With three drums batá a conga y un bongó
we emerged from her womb
Tumbling in rivers of our arms legs torsos
are tiny drums shaped like cells
coded with the logic of goatskin
Y venimos a la tierra

We're summoned by the echo of memory
two twigs two spoons provide steady chatter
con los palitos dos cucharas
y un tambor
a drum crackles
klak-klo   klak-klo
as maraca guiro & chekeré provide steady laughter
chiki-chi-chee-chiki-chi-cha
chiki-chi-chee-chiki-chi-cha

Torsos snapping like clams
breasts licking the moist tabaco air
male/female
Throats bouncing to the rhythmic tradition of thunder
as feet respond to that laughter of chekeré
chiki-chi-chee-chiki-chi-cha
as arms mimic the quest to grab lightning
as you & I huddle to double-check
if we're in the same moment
as everyone forgets the maddening hum
of common dust
at least for now
as everyone remembers the tradition

of birth in the pulse of a drum
as you & I compare the same copper skin
evidence of a similar rhythm
as you & I are summoned
to share the same memories—

Those drums are committed
are relics
for & de that space
where rumba had its crib
Legacy of aboriginal cane cutters
traders in spice
the deathly odor
of salted meats
Sweat si & yes
that humidity
that humidity ruffled by the sun

Bongó conga clave
cajón
these are breathing
museums of two cultures
these are the autochthons
of tone
of rhythm
of speech

That man leaning on a corner
that woman undulating in a river
that child standing at
a crossroads with
a steel crown
they have not forgotten
the echo of the batá
chiseled into cement sculptures

of hooded monks
Cobblestone roads hot
as July asphalt
bien caliente because today
September 8th
today tumbadoras are fondled
for La Caridad del Cobre
known around Belen as
Oshun

Those festivals in plazas presided
by the king Chano Pozo
his fingers aflame
slurrin' hymns in Lukumí
Abakuá
Lukumí Arará
raspy rum wails
Negras with long yellow
skirts copper bracelets
dancing a sensual shake
twinkling their eyes
in a heavy African ogle
cooling honey dew drops
with fans of peacock feather

Chickens & roosters walking their struts
oblivious to their sacred blood
Church & jungle symbolized
Seville & Ilé Ifé ritualized
Those rumberos will not
forget that marriage arranged
on high seas

A new identity writ
in ominous swells   A new
breed of troubador
Esas negras will continue
the snapping sway of hips
the tremble of thighs
to the crisp leather
crackling wood
their union
bonded by fingers aflame
responding to burning tongues

Amazing the first tún-tún!
Did Chano Pozo inherit
he whose ears were present
at the first drumming?
Astonishing the first callus!
Oye Chano
are your hands homesick
when not beating on goatskins?
Sobering the first sting of rum!
There are some
who say they saw
his birth in Belen
Some say he wore colored collares/necklaces
so his congas
could commune with deities
Some even say he baptized rumberos
with rum

Oye Chano
did you have calluses
the size of coconuts?
Did you
wear collares
when you
breathed yr
last sigh?

PULLING THE MUSE FROM THE DRUM

We petitioned the four directions
asked that their brother thunder
their sister lightning
escort us on a stroll
around architecture of goatskin y wood
Escort us on a quest
to pull the muse from the drum

The relation between drum & tongue
was there
when the mythic word
heard its first dialogue
between seven thunder 'n seven lightning
something about cedar
wanting the charm of speech
wanting to charm speech
The union was there
when the first word
the first drum
imitated sighs from jungles
a repartee
witnessed by jubilant stars

When chiefs 'n princesses
were traded for spice & steel
chained & herded unto Spanish galleons
How ominous to watch from a bush

sons of Felipe or Charles
iron vested men stalking
the Ivory Coast

～

Drums with thunder's spirit
embedded in wood
(ashé olubatá)
had to stay
yet memory brought the word
the song
ashé olubatá
there was a rebirth
of sound

Rhythms arrived hidden in pageantry
of scars & piercings
Soon it was decreed
that no drummings
tóques de tambor
will be allowed
for it was a known fact
drums excited people
Masters did not want property
to rebel
drum became whisper of rebellion
tongue of freedom
so feared by Spain

Yet wood & goatskin
continued their speeches

discretely in Caribbean jungles
The language of hands hide & cedar
could not be silenced
the ancestor's mother tongue
thundering who they were
where they come from—
Oko Iyesha mo ilé mi
Iya mi ilé odo
was their muse
was their poem

We hear the sound of history
through stained walls in Little Havana
grafitti parks Lower East Side
frozen lake Wicker Park Chaaiitown
grooooved into people's struts
It is you
It is me
It is
we
unidos Latinos
A collection of feathered drums
red & white
repicando
We pulling the muse
from the drum
the muse that is we

TO THE RHYTHM FAMILY
QUE ES OLODUM (BRAZIL)

Twa ilúlú
oyireo oyireo u
Twa ilúlú

Go into the head of rhythm
children of Olodum-mum-tum
The family
familia from
descendants de
Olodum meaning
for the drummer who communed directly-ti-ti
straight to the ears of Shangó—
Dios God Olodum-mum-tum
Synonyms in a tongue with no words
spoken with a són con tu pulso/pulse
their alphabet assembled with cowhides
with more mas mo' logic
el tún-ro-ko-tún always proved
one plus one does not equal two

From the northeast of Brazil
Bahia Salvador
from tribes that blended with Amazonian cacao
brown & around pythons
from Portuguese/Portugal anormal colon-
ization
importing Fon   Ashanti   Ewe
Yoruba   Nago

mining with cupped hands
gold/aurum/oro in the river Narciso/sus
never saw
From this the red the brown the black
Iberian DNA
friend of dominó
historically from cero-zero
to el doble-nueve
From this legacy
comes tattooed on clouds swirling
hymns of thunder
to bring you soft memories
of the toothless bearded
negríto bembón
priest/padrino in yr past life Ifa
The rhythm in unison with candomblé
twa ilélé
hypnotic samba tropicalismo
style
green style
tapping into the aboriginal ear
that possess even ancient spirits
they want to chiki-chiki
start creation myths otra vez
two fish doing a sweaty
horizontal lambada

Go into the head of rhythm
enter the realm where sound & trance
are twins of winds
rhythm & reason brother seasons
from the Amazon to Sudan

Be careful familia Olodum
Be rhythm
Be history
Be cultural memory—
iré ariku shé alafia eni—
be safe
for the rhythm family que es Olodum
does a beeline straight to the source
a projectile of surdo drums & marimba
snare & timbales
gods don't approve of borrowing sound
son sonido oido
from humans
tán-tán
so so
sabroso!

MUSIC & GUARACHAS WHEN
STORIES SOUND TOO TALL

Brothers & sisters
gente santa
enough of bogus stories
the moment has come
for a guaracha

Warm rain drums on dancing pavements
seeming as if roads
were puffing
tabaco smoke at the rain
Their union puffing
rings of hope their
union playing a furious
clave: one-two
one   two-three
took-took
took   took-took
That sonorous groove
infecting even chickens
Cuba with her rumba
infecting even sugar cane
Santo Domingo with merengüe
infecting even the coquí
Puerto Rico with her plena

The ominous clouds of darkened cotton
ask some questions
These islands have been children

of-the-north
islands children
of-the-east
These islands have a legacy of leaving
to-the-north
the-east
to-the-north
the-east
The motion is circular
Those oak sticks clack
Those maracas shoosh
The sound is circular
The clave goes
took-took
took   took-took

Enough of bogus stories
the moment has come
for a guaracha
We summon from the wood of cedar
from the hides of goats
the hope
that clouds once again
swirl in pearl formation

El pueblo's legs & hips
shoulders earthquaking to
congas bongós maracas guiro chekeré
Trumpets & trombones
singing with voices of rum
throats drinking melodies with mutes
gangs of cuatros strumming gypsy wails

truly a symphony of what we are
blood sand & tar

Amidst the embrace of the motherland
colonies we survive
a granddaughter of Yoruba slaves
with her skirt entices the wind
stirring hymns
of three rhythms
A northern breeze buries three
rhythms in clay
Yet people are drunk with that trancing
took-took
took   took-took
if only for a while
Because la gente remember
countless cocos & caracoles
dug from the muddy feet
of cotton trees
which then began to speak
Because in that clay
will sprout a rhythm
inspiring clouds
to once again
swirl in creole pearl formations

Enough is said
basta ya de cuentos
el momento has come
brothers & sisters
for a crazy
g   u   a   r   a   c   h   a

"THE BREEZE IS WIND BUT THE HURRICANE IS ALSO WIND"

. . . a Lukumí saying

for Victor Hernández Cruz

1.

Was today going to be
the day
we'd obtain wisdom
from the cool breeze?

2.

Clouds were quiet
as a tender eastern breeze
dried thick drops of sweat
from bodies now resting
under the red flowers of un flamboyán
the umbrella of a ceiba
dreaming ways of shelter
from the lions in the sky
a god with omnipotent lungs
Hurakán
We wonder if the growl of wind
will become a child's sigh
or tremble a far off Atlantis
pillars of salt
iodine caverns
cities that lost their witnesses
We ask if that snarl
will bend unknown palm trees

Rainbows have gone into exile
Hawks have abandoned
their peninsulas of straw
The flora is less adamant now
Leaves are serenely reading
their last rites
arranging funeral processions
They know when clouds sketch themselves
in true surrealist fashion
complete with blinking eye
& green lightning
they know
an artist will soon paint them
brown
paint them
crumbled
Trunks will bend into weeping figs

Biscayne Bay with all its tanned seaweed
floating coconuts y plastic bags
is now flustered like
spooked sardines
The bay is suspicious why tonight
there's a bottle of Bahamian rum
floating as well

3.
Shelters are full
Miami Beach is desolate
Hats toupees are securely fastened
Dade County shrieks in nervous jest
then is hush as a terrorized city

waiting for the first shelling
in a war between sky 'n ground
Cigars & glasses of water placed
at every door
Myrrh incense basil puff good fortune
Rattlers y maracas are shaken to scare
Hurakán

Hhhhooooo-hhhhooooo sh-sh-sh-psh!!!
BOOM!
Crrrraaack!!!
That ceiba tree wails
as she's tugged by her roots
Taka-taka-rrraka-taka!!!
Windows vibrate taka-rrrrraka-taka
machine-gunned by that blinking eye
Vultures knocking frantic beaks
on doors unexpectedly
BANG!   BANG!   BANG!!!!
A flying motorcycle
ghost-rides
into the side of a truck
etc., etc. . . .

The relentless bombing
continues until sunrise
Hurakán's sister
that queen of gust & grave
has begun to collect
her rage is eased
something about her lover thunder
being imprisoned

A dimmed sun oozes into
living rooms with no roofs
A child sits on a rocking chair
like a doll taunting evil spirits
her eyes bulging
like the fish at her feet

4.
The sun is now pinpointing
where pieces of lives
snaps of history are strewn
Monday is here wrapped
in a giant tear
This is a graveyard of memories—
clocks have melted
pictures are asleep
yet there is color
as if a myriad of brushes
had been jerked

The cities are bereft of flickering neon
as a sun with a necklace of bones
brown & black beads
says adios
There are enough tears
to power the stars that are watching
And dusk has decided to be maestro
of a symphony of insects
(It is quiet)
Frogs converse in croa-croa
Mosquitoes whistle around ears ankles
but don't sting

because even they
have compassion
(It is quiet)
Leaves are having their wakes
the grass is growing

And somewhere en el barrio
two hands play a distant clave
Suddenly a neighbor named Tito
joins with a bongó
pla-kee-plee pla-kee-plee-plak
Clave & bongó are speaking now
(It is quiet)
Then a few congas
join in the conversation
Ramón nicknamed Mongo
makes one drum say
kum-ma-kingking kum
plak-ki-plak
the others provide steady chatter
Cowbells & maracas
jump in
Soon the neighborhood has left
their battery-powered radios
their dwindling candles

They
have been summoned by rhythm
An old man Platanito
creeps his way into the source
He pulls from a black tattered case
a tarnished silver trumpet

Ese Platanito bloooows y bloooows
The drums speak louder
Cowbells scream a furious ting-ting
as Platanito bloooows
y que nota sopla ese Platanito
& everybody's feet are at least
twitching
because el barrio has realized
that the soothing breeze
is wind
but so is the hurricane
It is the price we pay
for living in paradise

CANCIONCITA PA' LA CEIBA/
SONG FOR THE SACRED MOTHER TREE

The ancient Lukumí
swimming in clouds of cotton
used to say
Eluayé ni mo se o Eluayé mi baba
Eluayé ni mo se o Eluayé mi baba
Obatalá ta wi ni wi ni se kuré
Araba iya

When the gentle trade winds
speak
when they consult the ceiba tree
on matters beyond their perceptions
she responds by twirling her leaves
like an alchemist does to dust from the heavens
she responds by directing her branches
as a Taino did to fish
towards the crossroads where
symbols that hold the key
to tomorrow's tears
or yesterday's fiesta
are about to arrive
on the wing of a wind
or the gust of a hawk

The ancient Lukumí used to say
when clouds were swimming in cotton
Eluayé ni mo se o Eluayé mi baba
Obatalá to wi ni wi ni se kuré

Araba iya
In African jungles she was teak
but when her children were
kidnapped
they could not bring her
aboard
ships whose wood squeaked the word
torture
so her children captured her strength
captured her power
& disguised it in the steel that bound them
the steel that killed them
She assumed a new identity
on her trip to a region
where mangos walk hand in hand
with guanábanas
& bananas relax on street corners
A region which an exaggerated breeze
brisa exagerada
named Hurakán
visits every summer & pens
a manifesto of destruction
Her name is now Silkcotton
that is
ceiba
Madre Ceiba
& Hurakán dares not
carve its name on her trunk

The ancient Lukumí used to say
when cotton was swimming in clouds
Eluayé ni mo se o Eluayé mi baba

Araba iya
as they circled the steps
engraved by ancestors shook-shaking
campesinos communing with
chanting to
mamita Ceiba
'round midnight
Those who in Matanzas
buried in her feet
cocos tattooed with tribal symbols
words wrapped in banana leaf
to inject them with magic
necklaces/elekes
bathed in riverwater
seawater
tabaco ash—
amulets against broken
rhythm

Here the air is pregnant with droplets—
water drops in
unannounced
we are all expectant mothers
waiting for the air to burst
So we ask mamita Ceiba
to shelter us from
heaven's tears
as we watch the years
in a lake
dance like a holy wave
a deeper shade
of cha-cha-cha—

the dance that put the lid on the jar
the dance like her leaf
the dance like her branch—

saludos a la madre Ceiba
Araba iya o

The Cantos

———————— ✦ ————————

"The most beautiful thing we can experience is the mysterious. It is the source of all true art and science. He to whom this emotion is a stranger, who can no longer pause to wonder and stand rapt in awe, is as good as dead."

—Albert Einstein

THE CANTOS

I.

Who was the first person to think
yr life was only yours—
how long did they last
& furthermore where did they go?

We say we can move the ground we walk
we say we do this bit by bit
We tap the earth with a twig torn
from the guayaba tree
We make sure what's in front
what's in back
moves & we say
this is not an illusion
not a trick
we do this poco a poco/ihérehére/bit
by bit
We make sure those 2 1 children at the corner
skip & sing jingles
we do this by sprinkling palm oil/
corojo at their feet
poquito a poco poquito a poco

There are many sidewalks in any city
but everyone eventually goes home
eventually opens a tiny door or drawer
or delivers a message

eventually bows to what will be
to what's going on
or what has been
Everyone eventually goes home

~~

Miguel Manguera y Antonio El Bembón
who defined the act of brotherhood
were standing on opposite corners of la bodega
They often boasted how nothing
could distance them
On a certain Monday
a boy with an old man's face
strolled down the street
wearing a tall phallic-shaped hat
half red half black
He walked by once whistling a tune about two friends
then twice whistling the same riff
& on the third stroll
Manguera wandered over to Bembón & asked what
is this viejito up to
walking back & forth & back
with a huge black
cone on his head
And Bembón said "Black!
Nononono I saw an old man but with a red
hat!" "Red hat!
That viejito's head was black!"
Manguera y Bembón kept arguing launching
smoking vowels
vowels of ashes

until fists legs sticks bottles
began to
stones began to fly
Meanwhile the old-man-boy
sat on the curb laughing in spurts
Bembón y Manguera noticed the character's sense
of humor
For a moment stopped fighting
ran across the street & growled
"Oye chiquitín
so it was you
who played the trick
& triggered this clash"
But the cone hat said
"I did not do such a thing (ha-ha!)
I was merely having my daily stroll (ha-ha!)
You see
the wise mothers & elders look
behind all the angles
You see (ha-ha!)
my hat is both red
and black"

❧

Eventually a flap of dried palm fronds/
raffia/mariwó hangs at yr entrance
Many bushes challenge yr courage
some even whistle
A flap dangles red
when you enter black
when you depart

Don Masayá had chiseled above his door
"Never
follow your footsteps"

Sometimes people shed that patch of mud &
opt for a forest of cement
shed that patch of cement &
opt for a city of mud

Some time had passed before
Don Masayá shed his fertile river
if only temporarily
We've wondered if he saw the black of flaps
or the red of fronds on his exit
He always says he will return
but through another door
another drawer
And he does this while wearing
a red & black cone hat
he does bit by bit
and he does this
not for the hell of it . . .

Most people misplaced
the language of taping the road
of whistling like a flute
of fishing fruit with little hooks
Don Masayá stands at the corner

A drawer with a knob of palm oil
greets his feet
A giggle spills
Hands clap in spurts
The breath
whistles a tune with sugar cane
Eventually everyone recalled
The scent of a messenger
combined with words of tabaco smoke—
yet this was the smell of home

II.

They said
do not return quickly
from a place
that requires
patience

They cleared a path through the woods
with a saxophone machete
Back in the 40s
back in the 30s
they slit the dog's throat
& listened to its whistle
Smoking melodies from brass
clearing the path with a machete de trompeta
Mario y Machito with machetes of sound

This
is what happened on the day those
wrapped with white cloth summoned
several blacksmiths
The clothing claimed the gulf was full of
bamboo y bushes
Who would forge certain tools
maybe some chains
to gap the gulf
between this wet land & that
island Who
would act the explorer the day
someone smithied a large knife

This was the death of dense bush
The seeded earth would be sewn
y soon there was more obstruction
The song of knives would need to
clank

Everyone had to pay the dues due
had to play that   diana-diana
diana-diana-diana
play it sharp
before entering the marketplace "Bodega"
There was always a dog at the gate
there was always a dog about to
salivate
awaiting yr entrance

❧

Don Masayá was a boy
when his father fanned the fires
that forged that large knife/
cuchillo
They were there
Masayón y Masayá were there
witnesses of nothing to something
among flora fauna y beehives
witnesses of the oaths sealed with 7 spikes on a railroad
Yet the boy already had been seduced
by basil   blood   &   honey
enamorado de sangre   albahaca   y   miel

❧

We temper art like patience
like Masayá would later write a
hammer hoe or chisel
deep in the jungle of his home—
like he would consecrate oaths con nosotros
singing standing like a spike with machete in one
hand
a family of trains on his shoulder—
like he always told us
he'd return then leave then return
descending on a chain
like DNA

～

They smithied a message on white cloth
signed it with honey & basil
They said: "give us a brush a pen
drums or a chekeré
the path will take you there . . ."
signed "M & M"
So the gulf was narrowed
with machetes of sound
So it was draped in white cloth
Mario y Machito lit the Afro-Cuban
& smoke the jazz
The artists promised access
to words on the chain
link by link
to the tune of the dancing knife
they said
dancing outside makes
thorns disappear

III.

The arrow was flicked by its owner
straight to the source
the source was a belly telling tales
spilling sweet wails of eternal return
at the feet of an almond tree
surrounded by vacant bottles of anise

If you set yr traps in the jungle
you must walk carefully
around the fauna
When you build yr boxes of steel
yr caves of paper
be cautious among the fauna
The accusations
the searchings
that fall short of their intended targets
they hover heavily over yr good hand

Sometimes you can arm yrself with
a pen as a bow
a tongue as a drum like a
verb is a bullet

Don Masayá flicked arrows of metaphor
(strickly from the oral)
to see on whose belly they'd land
Who would incite the first lie?
And was an arrow the quickest route around it?
This style of rainbows

rainbow's motion
trailed his words
like a particular accent
of heat mango conga y bembé

First you must puff libations to silence
invocations to stealth
There is enough static
enough exhaust
markets have become too big
the fruteros
la negra who sold ekó y cheketé
don't emanate from their albino cloth
the scent of sacred mysteries
Las antenas get jammed
our antennas se trocan

In the search for their footprints
one can slip like
when yr eyes dim
or yr staff rustles loudly
not to mention
they might've worn their shoes
backwards
(old Indian trick)
So you denounce with yr bows
blue & amber
& carry a quiver of memory
You dance among a circle
You pivot east west north south
You shoot yr metaphors yr myths
everything in $^{6}/_{8}$ rhythm

You make sure yr traps are hidden
yr traps have food
perhaps someone to witness the events
and most importantly:
(Don Masayá once said with a patch on his eye—)
avoid the hunter's
ultimate disgrace—
be discreet among the fauna

On our way home to the stretched earth
we saw a family of deer
by the hissing creek
We understood this to be an omen
of abundance
for the deer has many stories to tell
& a belly full
of metaphors

IV.

What is it about
he who walks with crutches
& falling skin
about people who fling
pennies at the floor even
cool coconut water to tame
his trails of dusty illness

Around these shores
we have not forgotten
how to read those signs
in between the flora
When strange tattoos begin to appear
on our backs our knees
we rush to make sure
that terra-cotta container & gourd
are still sealed still buried
among the leaves
the leaves should be intact

We also summon the androgynous healer
Rafael who
has the talent/ashé of trapping illness
with a coral & torquois fish net
while adding bits of river water
to seek the balance
because one hand cleanses the other
or they both remain stained

What is it about
he who walks with crutches
& falling skin
about people who fling
insults like a coconut in a storm
like y by bones bent into odd geometrical
shapes
like you are the chosen
who must walk this particular
street
Do you remember the last age when this was done?
You hope they at best tell you
to go to another land
for there
you'll at last be a king

In order to find the cure
we had to
enter el monte—
Oba ewé o awa ni ye ti wi ti wi
yo busca palo pa' curá christiano

Don Masayá spilled handfuls of toasted corn
showered certain trees with aguardiente
There was a shadow
whistling
which caused many a goosebumps
The figure wasn't
clear
but
with its one arm
pointed out leaves & roots

needed for the solution
Occasionally he spoke with a nasal song
staccato rhythm like
walking on
one leg
He had a small army of turtles following him
some in front
on his sides
some in back
They too now 'n then looked at us

Around these shores
we have not forgotten that
Uña de Gato & Cat's Claw
are the same immune builders
We've used Escoba Amarga
to sweep tumors & problems of skin
We tie a broom of Millo
behind the door
to halt the entrance of a plague
Caña Brava purifies an angry blood
Guaguasí smooths gashes
not to mention rheumatism y los intestinos
Salvia/Sage clears our headaches & clotted blood
like its smoke perfumes this room
Aloe is Sabila for those
who have swollen stomachs & kidneys
There is even
the roots of Aceitunillo (possible amulet)
for heads that think
too much

We arrived home
& went to see a beaded terra-cotta container & gourd
which slept at the feet
de una ceiba
We placed the herbs on top
& waited for instruction
while Don Masayá tapped the earth with an iron pole
that merged into a bird on top
A voice as if coming from Don Masayá's stomach
gave us the prescription—
a decoction for seven days at six a.m.
before any meal
Always pour a bit
on top of the gourd—
(y vamo a vé)

Those signs often say
to spill words into the solution
the infusion will cleanse
tilt the imbalance
circle it like a fish net
& drape a lid of purple & burlap cloth

Los signs often say
that word ordains it
(y vamo a vé)

V.

Several melon seeds seeds of
    calabash
        were strewn in dance towards the end
            of our migration
For the guajiro who arrives & reverently tips
at the teaming soil
        a sombrero of straw
pyramids of glass impose their difficulties—
the scent of manure is not equal to that of piss
a city's soil sprouts parking meters
        & not patches of malanga or ñame

Yet within a calabash you can build little worlds
        even feed newly arrived relatives
the ones with skin discolorations
      who've never had a birthday party
        (much less an honorary drumming)
who've never bitten into those northern apples
    whose cows often had translucent hides
      who've plowed with large tiles as chariots
    & an umbrella of sweat

    When markets echo
like voices from void stomachs
    the guajiro has
      the advantage
He greets his tomatoes
    like an old friend
      his pigs his cows his feathered cohorts

he shakes the leafy hands
            of spinach & lettuce
    not to say
            certain medicinal weeds
                who always ambush the scene

Two elders assembled
on Don Masayá's porch
            (custom of enlightenment)
They suggested trips to several spans
    of desolate dirt
            to search for Juvenál
                who had no wife
            nor children
They said he would be
            strutting by pregnant banana stems
        perhaps counting the ladybugs
Upon arrival Don Masayá should
        bury two coconuts along with a lilac-beaded satchel

Soil is hip to several secrets of
        transforming the mundane into story

He should shovel & hoe his
        memories of abundance
            spray a verse about journeys to forgotten farms
                let it land like bubbles
                    on the reddish sod
Eventually he would host a procession of
        beat & goatskin   dance & leaps
            into fields of distant trance
Juvenál would be annoyed at this festivity

Call the police
 Accuse Masayá of theft
  of burying stolen money
But Masayá would order
 an excavation of the trampled turf
All they would find will be two cocos
 in a bag of broken beads
For recompense
 Juvenál would concede
  y con seeds
   portions of the earth

The left hand was stretched deep
 into a pocket of soil
  Where were the elements needed
   at the end
    of our migration?
  Where were the elements needed
   that would prove this perennial?
Soon
 rows of yams y calabash would puff
  like ashes from those volcanoes
Memories of abundance
 sprouted into the present
  into poems regarding guajiros
 yet there were always
  laments
 about this new land
  or the hand forgetting to tip
   our sombrero of sweat

VI.

"We fumbled our ears
   like lazy chunks of flowing lava
      unto this here hill
   we heard certain gurgling
      molten stones cascading/
            cascadas
         de piedras
            enfurecidas
                  (otán iná)
   Bubbles of burbujas burbujas is bubbles
      panting rhythms of vapor
This was not just
   another display of tone
remember those rumblings
      from below
   windows that shook the landscape
      like a painting by Wilfredo Lam
         like a wave of a whip like
            when we heard that tribe of buffalo
               in a parade of tremors

But where is the image of the first hand
      that reached into a pouch of magma?
         Or was it always hidden
            inside an obsidian urn strewn
               in the volcano's jungle?
   This hand
this pouch of scarlet skin
   belongs to the courier the iron carver

drummer   dancer   the   minstrel   the   mother
        a lover a puta/whore
             healer/santero/shaman
               the suicide
           even the killer/matón
We crossed the gulf of empty boats
the bridge of water looking more like cemetery
    y si
        las cascadas gargled the same stones
                estas
           piedras
        otra
     vez!
This was evident
    when we summoned the remains of lava-like clay
        when the ground came roaring
            at our fumbled ears"
(Don Masayá once said while
    gazing through a trembling window
        the window carved like a hand)

VII.

This is only a greeting
short shout out to our sister
    to our helmet of calabash
    whose face is a calligraphy
    of red & white circles
    tiers of tears of chalk
    cascadas de cascarilla fúnfún
    hojas of rojo deep
    in the grooves of our heads
Our crown/adé beaded with glass
    ella with fountains of cowries crying like
    strands of four virgin tufts
    braided at that
    cocolo at that—
    Dada . . .

VIII.

Son los jimaguas son dos jimaguas
    (kere kere yan)
son los jimaguas son dos jimaguas
    (kere kere yan)——
bit by bit you see twins
become chiefs of scattered cliffs
hills shaped like practical jokes
sometimes a pebble
sometimes a stone
We see these twins become
patrons
of peculiar births
Esos with births peculiar
spill balls of candy——

Imagine
the river's surprise seeing
two children wrapped in rainbows
spring from her spring——
Bells gongs/agogo agó ting tunes in $^6/_8$

But todo el mundo
eventually loves a twin
people con their jimagua
their favorito
Idowú
even
if they were born
solo y solito

IX.

We purchased a piece of thunder
a ki-lak-um of ilú/tambor
We caught the thundercelt
in its rapid descension to
the dance of flames

We've seen the face of power
inside the inverted pilón
mortar con(secretos)
There were certain shadows
of caudillos on white horses—
Trujillo before his last date with the mistress
Batista entering one of his casinos
Barrientos posing with el Ché
Diaz Ordáz & corpses of 300 students
Videla surrounded by Plaza de Mayo mothers
Somoza slipping on a banana from United Fruit
Rios Montt wearing the cloth of countless massacred indios
Fidel is surfing the Gulf on a raft with his favorite cow
There were certain shadows
of the ceiba tree where they hung themselves
within the inverted pilón
mortar con(secretos)
After the tyranny
there are so few places to go
places to sing
eat gourds of kimbombó & kalalú
kalalú y kimbombó

We purchased a pinch of
kin-ki-lak kin-ki-lak kin-ki-lak
Who would be struck by red thunder
being summoned by goatskin?
And how would the first flame
arrive at the throne?
A palma showed us its kingdom—
we were smiling like red-vested mummies
like dancing worms
in a puddle of stones
pile of water
streams of smoke
smoke of streams sending signs
estamos vivito y coleando
this culture is still burning fresco
cool y caliente like guaguancó/columbia/yambú
Muñequitos de Matanzas style
like bomba y plena
Cepeda style
like merengue
Ventura style

There were certain shadows
of the imprisonment of Masayá
of the day he found Olufina's horse
on the path to the big mortar
on his way to greet
him
The horse had been missing for some time
But just as Masayá was approaching the throne
Olufina's guards saw riding the stolen horse
(ki-ti-tak ki-ti-tak ki-ti-tak)

saw him as a thief
(ki-ti-tak ki-ti-tak)
saw him prisoner
(kó-kó-kóóóó)
Don Masayá stated his case to small burned stones
He remained prisoner with a pen as a pillow
& white cloth
Yet mothers were giving birth to death
crops wilted the river
was now a snake of clay

A poet with yellow & green tongue & wrists beaded
told Olufina there was someone
wrongly wrapped in iron boxes
someone of some relation
This retribution
was the source of much trouble
Masayá would later brand a poem
unto the turtle's shell
offer it to Olufina—
". . . so long you kept me hidden
& never saw my face
When would you've realized that I
did not steal yr horse
that I came to yr land to greet you
& bring you a gift . . ."

El pueblo dice: Obakosó o
& drums summon thunder
dicen: Obakosó o
& stones rain from the sky
dicen: Obakosó o

& the caudillo dangles from a ceiba
dicen: Obakosó o
& the old memory is the new
dicen: Obakosó o
& the new memory crackles
dice Masayá: Obakosó o
& odu burns beyond

X.

1. COTTON

We are still arriving at this
side of the gulf
draped with white wool
Clouds of cotton lick our skin
this is after all
how we hope the year to swell
to be tutu atoned
These tufts of peace dangle
from our hands
We don't see them or
we forgot what they look like
but all we need to ting the memory
is the white hair of viejos y viejas—
they walked through the pewter door
with pelts of pearl goatskin above
it touched their heads
it was how they got that way
The story is true

2. FROM COTTON TO CLOTH

There were 16 windows with
panes of cotton tufts—
we saw them yawn like several wide fields soft
dented hills with cutlass on their apex
ceiba with a dove-shaped
treehouse
where the sun beamed through its eyes forming
two slowly sonorous circles

on the cloth floor
rhythm lazy like those
who live
by their wisdom

3. EWÉ

When your head is too hot
bathe under umbrellas of almond leaves
mucho/cha lime chalk
y chacho
be cooool
If the headache persists
trap a leaf of prodigiosa
inside yr white hat kufi or sombrero
(y pa' que fue eso!)

4. HAIKU FOR WAR

Has the time come for
sabers to ride his horse? But
where are herbs of truce?

5. SNAIL

Oye
it's not so much that the snail
carries a home on its happy trails
but that it does this
with patience
like clearing paths of broken rhythm
leaving a trail of luster
trail of wisdom

The first migrants brought
from the other world
sus tierras
wrapped in snail shell
some soil & spread the first mound
(fue la creation of criollos with hyphens)
They declared their space—
built hands to grip scrolls of joy
stir snakes of sadness
gather latters of serenity
quarter-moons of warriors
while the sun lit candles to compassion
We
did this
galloping
on a snail

6. CAUL

The kid was born
   in a caul the
      ruin shall be
         if they sprinkle hot
            palm oil on the head
      the shroud shall be sliced
         they will burn with the slightest tropical sun
            se acabó/adagbó
           salakó

7. LA VIEJITA CHISELS AWAY

One voice spilled its breath
into the womb

La vieja sat on her rocking chair
with the tail from her son's horse
With a mellow whisk
the butterflies circling her head
then danced towards that womb
as if they got the idea from her white hair
as if each flutter finished the sculpture
as if the sculpture was shaped in her head

8. ALBINO

We sat among large bleached stones littered
on the river with body
like snake
scales y todo
A bearded viejo with white guayabera
cane beaded nacar/pearl
eyes strung with clouds
swirled to our huddle
He said el rio no se rie
stones of honey don't spring their joy
fish y cocodrilos forgot the tradition
of oracles porque
baba mí remains inside an iron box
the box encircles peace & knowledge
but knowledge & peace must be free to
penetrate the cream color of our bones
The poem must tell y spell the story
words must dance with memory
our memory keeps
swelling
¿Sabes?

XI.

This story could take place
inside a caramel cave
large amber balls dangle faithfully
above the entrance where
there's a copper key
to another kingdom

She sat on the edge
    of her home
        stirring a bowl of amalá
She recalled the tale
    of her headtie &
        why
    it covered her ears—

Years had passed since she was married to a rumbero
& olubatá with one hand red the left white whose
sound was sublime whose rhythm smoked stones of
tones   But he was always off at some rumbón crack-
ing goatskin   He was never home never tranquilo
So she asked her good friend who had honey swim-
ming through her veins & was hip to such mysteries
to find a way to keep el sublime home el sublime to
herself   Her girlfriend suggested she cook him his
favorite dish of amalá   But instead of putting meat
she should cut off her ear (eh?) her ear cut off so he
will always listen to her   So she did this   And when
he came home sat down to eat he wondered why she
had a headtie covering even her ears   And what was

that stain on her left side anyways   El Sublime tore
the cloth from her head   He was horrified at the
empty hole & sent her off bien lejo   This is where
she stayed—away from most people

This could be a cave
where a lady who severed her ear
fed it to her husband
covers her ear everyday
to remember that she must be
heard

XII.

for Rene

She who is owner of the last breath
flows through pink & wine painted tombs
always that stage before
birth before
wind tumbles a destiny
into cupped hands
filled with river water
ready to be splashed on this empty womb

She who is owner of cemeteries
where the mist of memory
the ancestors sleep
is not disturbed
by the raucous of reason
Here we rest in a woven basket
among skulls & small bones
The laughter must be muffled
Muffled must be the music
solemn & serious
austere as the day she left to live
in the most hushed of homes
among epitaphs of bearded revolutionaries
poets with calluses
drummers with burning tongues
like the day she left
after that same drummer
with one hand red
the left white
rejected her braided hair with crown of bones & cowries

like when she danced with her back
departing from the drum
covered with white raiment
brocaded with tombs of immigrants
　　always that stage before
　　now the beginning of a new
　　gente
　　(Crioooollos)

XIII.

We whirled softly towards the gates
of this cemetery
armed with pods from poincianas/flamboyán
rattling like bones from old skeletons
enticing the wind to come & play
come 'n play
we do this carefully
around these peninsulas
she has a habit of suddenly
exhaling
gates slam open pods
knife the air like boomerangs
not to say mangos y aguacates
who often believe themselves BOMBAS
We do this carefully
many a times fierce women
women with hairdos like tornadoes
like branches from flamboyán
necklaces of buffalo horns hang
with snaps of hurricanes trapped
twist unto the scene
red pants buried
below rainbow branded skirts
skirts jingling 9 bells cascabeles
small knives hoes sickles etcétera

Amalia had a husband
whose head was so red
so hot he could ignite a bonfire

by spitting into a pit of cedar logs
As a result he had several scars
as testament to his habit of war
Once many of his enemies
surrounded Amalia's home
& demanded he come out
There was no way both of them
could fight them off even
if she opened a buffalo horn
Yet a gust of thoughts
breezed through her braids & red hair ties—
Amalia decided to dress her husband
in her multicolored pants
& sash of red raiment
even braid his hair
When the disguise was complete
this guy her husband bolted out the house
hopped on her horse & thundered past his enemies
like a mix of fire & gunpowder
His enemies still thought he was inside
until Amalia came out whirling softly
dressed in her usual
with a flywhisk/iruke beaded rusty
looking like the tail of a tornado
This really happened
And though Amalia & her husband
don't live together
(You see
two rams don't drink from the same fountain)
she is her husband's right hand—
though they don't live together—
he always leaps as if reaching for the source of lightning

& dances a smokin' rumba
when she wraps the rainbow
around her hips

XIV.

There used to be huge heaps of stones
seemingly round & burnt
awash on this shore: small
attempt at quenching the sea's hunger for tierra: this
was to maintain the ocean
chained to her floor to deep
volcanoes con valleys of masked fish
Many of us assembled on these stones
(the last hurdle before
the beginning of new criollos
before the lasting exodus
from island to island to peninsula
with arms half closed
elbows jagged)

on these stones: El Muro . . .
We/us/nosotros
often saw the memory of petitions floating
desolate:
cocos painted blue/añil
    seven watermelons twisting like escaped boats
        deep fried slices of platanos
            macitas de puerco
                even a rooster shedding its soaked skin
                    on its way to delivering a message of hope
                Strewn on the glassy sand we witnessed now 'n then
            several big black rubber doughnuts strung
        like a necklace of used coffins
torn clothing y todo

~

So we tossed silver tools into the froth of her skin
for balseros adrift with sails of quilted handkerchiefs
for immigrants stowed among cargo—
oars for motion & growth
a helm to steer their stay
anchor to firmly ground their roots
a life preserver so their memory survives
(salvavida)
upon reaching new shores upon new
criollos being born
pendant of a siren among stones in groves
siren to whisper secret psalms of history
African something something
       Spanish

~

Those who were whipped into ships
whose planks squeaked the word torture
whose peste reeked the noise   agony
whose treasures were never found
Those who made it across to
new lands to blend into soil
into las palmas las ceibas
cocoteros mango y mamey
into waves that peck & tumble these stones
into the blood of our hymns y poesia
tambor campana y chekeré

Those who returned to our mother's breast
which hung l
        o
           w
'till bursting into ocean

XV.

Prologue to a really long poem . . .
Para Jessica

Ladékojú ibu yí odo . . .
We see a five-pointed crown
brass with strands of amber dangling
basking atop stones on this riverbank
Cowrie shells blended jingling receiving messages
from fish spawning:
El rio se reía—
we hear laughter of currents kissing stones
Here
is where his mother lives:
these fish keep kissing our feet
as they paddle with brass oars
towards the source of abundance
we'll dance as if carrying a calabash of love
on our heads where we'll dance as if
our torsos were waves
shoulders were short ha-has of laughter
to rhythms in bells/chaworó
in drums/tambor/ibu aña
El rio se reía—
(laughter of currents kissing stones)
If it wasn't for the sh-sh-sh of water a
smooth splash of a calabash on her womb
rubbed with beeswax five ferns parsley y perejil
his mother would not give birth
there would be no continuity
this is how we always did it

the beginning trickles few stones y cowries
then gradually spreads 'till
the river is where we fish the tradition
the tradition flows from spring to town to town to
homes to ocean

She who shelters cinnamon skin
with long yellow raiment
silks embroidered with peacocks
She whose hair is braided with amber-sculptured fish
She whose wrists swivel brass bracelets
enticing even crocodiles to smile
even the lonesome ironsmith/Alagbedé
to leave his fort of leaves   trees & steel
to share his tools of creativity
trompeta   hammer & pen
machete y chisel
She whose eyes tear long streams of honey
who with a certain African ogle
ojo con sabor y meneo
has combed con miel the bodies of many lovers—

And she has a habit of
listening to bells y cascabel
below cascades then
fingering her hair to its rhythm
This can be her throne
Here is where these drops glisten
like little mirrors
like snaps of herself which when reach the ground
become her image
su cara de azucar marrón

Tribes of bees huddle & check themselves in the stream
make sure their yellow rings
blend with the pollen
their signature is still intact
while the queen cools herself with a tiny fan/abébé
of peacock feathers
waiting for her mirrors her people
to arrive
Here is where his mother lives
Don Masayá was taught to speak of himself like

"I was born on a riverbank
embraced by honey-soaked stones/
(oñi sokuta)
The spring that sprung gourds of compassion
of laughter of cinnamon twigs
was my womb
I was born on a riverbank
between humidity & drizzle
while my father was working
forging some sort of art"

XVI.

for the memory of Miguel Febles

We see
thin brass chain
8 snaps of turtle shells
laced
suspended on this palma
between palm nuts ready
to tumble & spin the past
into words of tomorrow

This is to poet what pen is to diviner
This is to diviner what pen is to poet

They cast words into
hoodoo rhythms palabras con ritmo y tún-tún
cast words unto wooden tray with
mobius signs of energy & elephant
Circles begin to whirl
las hierbas suddenly exude
liquid consciousness
stones bounce down the river of tradition
tongue touches bones with tones of wisdom

We see
thin brass chain
8 snaps of turtle shells
laced
suspended at the beginning of a poem
we assembled to hear

They said
whoever chants like whoever owns black-
sewn gourd with tongue inside white-
sewn gourd with tongue inside
has the gift of camaleón
pivoting eyes etcétera or
hangs like a bat who
upside down sees everything below the surface or
sits on a straw mat coiled
able to sense the essential heat or coolness of cells
like the flick from a python
sitting on a straw mat coiled

They said
this is to poet what pen is to diviner
this is to diviner what pen is to poet

We summon poems from past figures
spirits with green & yellow pens
flowing wrists
who tossed brass chain
laced
with little poems who
spoke regarding our people's seat
where to sit
where it sat &
what to do once we found it
(Yoko obi yo ko obi   [CALL]
Ayal'awo yoko obi yo ko obi ayal'awo   [RESPONSE])

へ〜

If it wasn't for 16 verses/odu
mutating to 256
to thousands
we would not know
(canto que canta la story/history
of who we are spoken in rhythm)
The child who performs feats with jest
opens doors & drawers which always lead home
The first owner of steel who cleared the path
with machete of sound
danced outside to our music
to make thorns disappear
The one who throws arrows of myth & metaphor
lands quickly killing a belly full of lies
Healer who undulates in cool green water
healer with crutches & falling skin
who owns sickness who owns the cure
Campesino who's hip to secrets of soil
The one with wine colored sash
who carries a slight tremble of earth inside
Our sister with strands of virgin tufts
who watches ibeji/twins/son los jimaguas son los jimaguas
(kere kere yan)
make sure they get their marbles & candy
Her brother the rumbero with charm
who speaks in goatskin & dance
like a ki-lak-gun of drum
& has a bit of tyrant in him
El viejo y la vieja with eyes strung like clouds
royal in their beaded canes
She who hides in caves & is missing an ear no one spoke to
She who lives in trenches of chastity in cemeteries

She who is armed with tornadoes in her skirt pods from flamboyán
She who piles round stones in ocean
mothers our journey from island to isla to land
She who laughs like currents kissing stones
flows with cinnamon skin on a riverbank sweet
& carries the calabash of love
He who sits on a straw mat coiled in
white raiment
sensing the essential heat or coolness of cells
summoning which came before then
spraying words
to give energy its form

We see
thin brass chain
8 snaps of turtle shells
suspended on the hand that writes the hymns from our homes
that asks the piercing questions
that spills the answers from memory
that divines the poem
Don Masayá was witness
to prophecy coming to pass
They said he was to be born
among honey-soaked stones
They said
he would have a gentle
character cool y soothing
like a slight smile
father of the mysteries of verse

Mis Gente

"El que no tiene de Congo tiene de Carabalí."

—popular Cuban saying

The sacrifice was made
They said frijoles, fish, coco
corn con kimbombó/amalá   akará
café   tabaco y ron
honey to sweeten the journey
The cloth depicting rainbow's creation
A bundle of 21 branches
they said each has ashé——
tiene cuatro viento
tiene thunder
tiene tierra
tiene agua (ocean y river)
tiene sombra y shade
tiene sting of steel that cut them
This was draped with 9 candles & 2 roosters
white
as well
They said: Ilé mo ku o   [CALL]
                   Akueyé   [RESPONSE]
                   Ilé mo ku o   [CALL]
                   Akueyé   [RESPONSE]
                   Egun mo ku o   [CALL]
                   Akueyé   [RESPONSE]
                   Obi Egun   [CALL]
                   Akuaña   [RESPONSE]
They said: Eyeife——
This is how it was done
We do it this way
The blood spilled

will be blood giving life
the food spread like a fan
his nourishment
the cloth his skin
branches his bones

The wavy thread will now continue
flickering dripping
as well

They said: Iboru Iboya Iboshishé—
His birth was
like this

MOKONGO Y TO' ESA GENTE

Eyibaríba eyibaríba nkamá   [CALL]
Wá   [RESPONSE]
Eyibaríba eyibaríba nkamá   [CALL]
Wá   [RESPONSE]
Sounds that spread through past wombs
those before Mokongo y toda esa gente
sound too much like thumps
like the procession of feet from Abakuá
on that day carrying casket y bailando la caja
teetering on bounce of $^6/_8$ rhythm
like an incomplete thought between bone & spirit—
we were born on a such a day
on such a day we kneeled before certain clouds
& chose our calabash full of destiny
The hardest thing to remember
are sounds from those wombs before Mokongo—
Eyibaríba eyibaríba nkamá   [CALL]
Wá   [RESPONSE]

Four years he wandered streets in Regla
lingering like delicate webs of tabaco smoke
or inside vacant bottles de aguardiente
(That's why bottles should be laid to rest while empty)
Even two miscarriages our mother had
So they clipped a bit of ear from the stillborn
to identify him indelibly upon return
y to assure he did not leave again
fastened small chain around left ankle
After four years Mokongo y toda esa gente

decided to help
On such a day
we sealed the pact with death/iku
iku would have to filter through thick curtains of raffia
though the sounds thumped like a procession of feet
against the ear missing a snap—
Eyibaríba eyibaríba nkamá   [CALL]
Wá   [RESPONSE]

༄

What about Feyo, Frank, Emilio, Luis, y Mongo
their hair their platinum teeth
how they were men y mostly fathers
one young guerillero leaning on steel bars
shot in Santo Domingo
They keep waving flags of rainbow
asking for glasses of water
flores y perfume
claiming they're still here—
though de vez en cuando
some café spills prior to being served
or a plate with morsels of platanos arroz y pollo asado
cracks in approval like an offered eucharist

And how can we forget Alfonsa y Atandá
placed like a dune of stone on the shore
smiling like someone who's known you for a while
dress of blue gingham/guinga
white fila flapping
like waves of laughter

In an isolated house
a father remains alone wearing
milky silky slacks y guayabera
watching the Mediterranean stucco & tile
asking certain stones & ceiba
wind & stream who animate things through the
other world
to deliver this message to his son
We need the skull of a ram carnero o sheep—
just like bone is past memorized
just like blood is life actualized
so is spirit time humanized

Eyibaríba eyibaríba nkamá   [CALL]
Wá   [RESPONSE]
Eyibaríba eyibaríba nkamá   [CALL]
Wá   [RESPONSE]
Tó Egungun!

Two years had passed and I still couldn't find work. After Batista put a new tax on the tanning industry, a lot of factories went out of business; including the one I had been working at for the last year or so. I had nothing to do. And it wasn't that I didn't want to work. It was that at the time in Cuba the old colonial Spanish mentality towards work pervaded. Old people had priority in jobs. Once you got hired you could not be fired unless you were caught stealing or something like that. No one would hire young people until an older person either retired or died. And there was usually a long long waiting list of people waiting for a position to open. This was especially true in the shipping docks, which was the principal industry in Regla. A lot of people made good livelihoods from loading and unloading those huge cargo ships. So being un jovencito I was stuck. ¡Imaginate! Two years without working! I was desperate. So I said, bueno, me voy para los Estados Unidos.

I managed to get my stepfather Mongo to loan me $100. Oye, $100! Cien pesos en esos tiempos! That was for many people a month's salary. And Mongo, although obviously not a young man, was also unemployed. He made a living in the meantime hustling and trading boxes of rum (usually stolen) for contraband American cigarettes. So he gave me the money to come to the U.S. under the condition I pay him back when I could.

There was a black-and-white passenger/light cargo ship that departed every Friday from the port in La

Habana to Miami. She was called the "Florida." Forty dollars would get you across the Florida Straits. So that day, January 18, 1954, I packed my little maleta with all my clothes— two pants, four shirts, five or six underwears, a couple pairs of socks, and a sport coat. That was it. I said goodbye to Mima and Mongo, to my brothers and sister, some friends; snuck away from Rosa my ex-wife who was still after me, and went aboard the ship. It was just about sundown. Six o'clock or so. Si six o'clock because I remember the ship departed at six sharp. And as luck would have it a cold front was setting in so the seas were going to be rough.

This boat was no dinghy. We're talking pasajero y de carga. And I tell you the "Florida" was diving in and out of the surf at the mercy of the waves. I gotta admit, I was a bit scared. A bit no. ¡Tenía un miedo del carajo! I remember even singing un cantico to Yemayá hoping she would calm the seas. But in any case, el barco made it to the Port of Miami, which in those days was on the Miami River, just upriver from Government Cut, at about six in the morning. No one was hurt. Just a lot of seasick individuals. I, gracias a Dios, didn't get sick. Although I had never before been on a ship, I had been on many boats before, especially the ferry boat brom Regla to La Habana.

6:00 A.M. January 19, 1954. The day I first stepped on United States soil.

The breeze was kind of cool. The cold front was already settling in. The sky was very cloudy. Like rain, como un día de lluvia. There I was literally just off the boat and standing on the docks like in a hex wondering what next. I spoke no English. And in 1954, nobody spoke Spanish in Miami. This was a cracker-town. And I mean a town. Miami was very small in those days. There was hardly even a downtown. The only thing I knew how to say was "I go to Cuba." And this I said when I wanted to tell someone where I came from. So that's to give you an idea of the extent of my English. I wanted to get something to eat but I didn't know where to go. I didn't know how to go to downtown or anywhere for that matter. Not only that, the food that was available was food I didn't recognize. And I wasn't going to risk spending that little money I had on something I didn't know whether I was going to even be able to eat, not to mention the possibility of indigestion. I walked around the dock for a little while, trying to talk to people, to see if I could find some work. But it was too difficult to try to communicate in sign language. Keep in mind nadie hablaba español. No one could direct me to where I could find work. I realized real quickly that Miami was not somewhere I should stay. So I decided to find a way to get to New York.

I found out there were two trains running from Miami to New York City. The "Champion" and the "Silver Star." The "Champion" arrived in New York City in something like 22 hours, while the "Silver Star" took a couple of hours more. But more important, the "Silver Star" was cheaper—$41. So I caught that train that evening. It was to arrive in Penn Station at midnight the next day.

And so there I was, a Cubanito just off the boat, hadn't eaten in over a day (I didn't eat on the train because I couldn't order anything and didn't know the prices, and again I didn't want to risk spending what little money I had; all I drank was a pint of milk), speaking no English, in Penn Station, at midnight, mid-January, and only a sport jacket to keep me warm. I asked some people how I could get to 1057 Bergen Street. I would show them the wrinkled piece of paper where the address was written. But in Manhattan no one that I asked, or could understand what I was saying, knew where Bergen Street was. Finally someone suggested I take a taxi. This man charged me $19 to take me to Bergen Street in Brooklyn. That left me with just a few dollars; less than 10.

Bergen Street was the home of some distant cousin from my mother's side. My sister Nilda was also in Brooklyn but I didn't know where. So Bergen Street was my only haven. I arrived around 12:30 A.M. at my cousin's house. Needless to say he was very surprised. He let me in. I told him my situation. That I needed a place to stay until tomorrow. That I hadn't eaten in over a day and only had a few dollars left 'till I found a job. His wife graciously prepared me something—I think it was arroz con ropa vieja. I knew he owned a restaurant so I asked him if he could hire me to do dishes or mop the floor or whatever. He told me he had sufficient help. And just as easily, without even blinking, told me I couldn't stay with him for the night. ¿Tu te imagina eso? ¡Ni una noche me pudo hospedar! Pero bueno, at least he referred me to some people from Regla who in turn knew where my sister was staying. I slept there for the night and the next day I met up with Nilda. Turned out she was renting a room in an apartment that belonged to an elderly Cuban man. And she would cook and clean for him aside from the factory job she had as an undocumented alien (she would later get deported back to Cuba). I stayed with her until I got settled in a job.

The very next day I went into Manhattan to find a job; wearing my only sport jacket. Can you picture this Cubanito going into Manhattan on train y solo? I got so lost! It took me all day to get back to Brooklyn. But nevertheless the next day I went at it again armed with my residency card. Ya yo era residente. (In those days all you needed to get your residency was to go to the American Embassy in La Habana, say you wanted to go to the U.S. to work, say that you had some money saved up—I said $1,200—and you wanted to put it in a bank account or invest it, and they would promptly give you your residency card. That was it. No proof required.) I couldn't tell you how many places I asked for work. I would ask, "Chob fo' mi?" Every factory turned me down. There were times when I thought, "Coño, is this country as difficult as it seems? Isn't this the land of opportunity? Because if it is, opportunity is *not* knocking at my door." I figured if I couldn't find a job soon, I would simply go to immigration and ask to be deported. But someone thankfully referred me to a General Electric cable factory. They, gracias a Díos, hired me. I was reaching the end of the line as they say. Tenía la soga en el cuello. By the way guess what was the first thing I bought with my first paycheck.

Claro que si! A long thick green coat with fur on the collar. So anyway I stayed working there for 8 or 9 months. I received several monthly promotions in salary. Me fué bastante bien. I always made more cables than the quota. You see, I always worked more than necessary.

Two years after being in New York City I went back to Cuba for a visit. I offered to pay Mongo the $100 he loaned me. But he refused to accept it. He had a job already, las cosas had changed. He refused to accept it.

It was still early in the morning, como las seis. The colonel with shiny silver teeth was being driven through town in one of those khaki army cars. Las calles were still silent with the hiss of terror. But already I was on my way to school on Estrelleta Street en El Malecón. The car eased into a slow groove like an old man carrying the load of years. They said, "Mira niña, como te llamas? Donde tu vives? Quienes son tus padres?" This shoot-out of words came after the indecent whistle which shattered my glassy ears. They wanted to know where I came from. I told them. As I finished my sentence, it began to rain drops of silver, small pieces of furniture, baskets of frutas, guayabas & everything, even a wedding gown. I was fifteen. Within a month I would not see my mother for several years. I was forced to marry the sergeant riding in the passenger-seat. He liked me. Period. He bought me. Period. My mother had to, in effect, concede, or she would go to prison. This happened to our neighbor Maribel. This was why Mamá wanted to come to the north. Mamá dreamt this scenario happening to me. Silver teeth y everything. She could not sell me to one of Trujillo's boys. She would go to prison before doing that.

ᘓ

Mamá came first with my sister Clara who was still a baby. They arrived at what is now Kennedy Airport on a flight from Puerto Rico at midnight, November 5th, 1952. Even then it was like a beehive of jets buzzing toward the land of honey-coated dollars. Stratosphere liners shaped like dollar signs. She was handed samples of odors from New York. A snap from an old sewing machine. Two subway tokens. A murky glass of water which was at one time grimy snow. It did not however smell like piss. She was handed the tip from a slice of pizza, a cardboard container of fried rice, still-crisp matzoh, a dried seasoned leaf of calagreens; she already knew about the red beans. Edna Bom, born in Curaçao, was married to a Dominican man. She had these samples in her memory. Her memory said that in fact pavements were paved with opportunity. Mamá soon discovered how selective those memories were. I would say she was the one who convinced Mamá to come. It sure wasn't my stepfather Feyo. He had a good job crunching numbers for Chrysler and had no interest in leaving the country. He thought Mamá was overly preoccupied with Trujillo's boys stealing one of her daughters. Well, Feyo & Mamá got divorced. He stayed. Mamá lived in this honeycomb filled with many other imported bees and struggled like one for two years. All the while she sent bits of honey-coated dollars back to Santo Domingo in order to maintain us. We (my older sister Luisa & younger brother Frank) stayed at a rooming house with my father. After two years Mamá returned to Santo Domingo to take us back to New York. We had an interview with an official at the American Embassy in la capitál. But Luisa, with her turbulent temper, insulted the official. Don't ask me how or why. The room was so muffled with the sounds of shuffling papers & pencils snapping. He said that as long as he worked in the embassy he would personally see to it that we were never allowed in the U.S. There was only one other escape hole. So Mamá took us to Venezuela. Luisa & Frank were sent to New York only after a month or so of being there. They stayed at my oldest brother Nelson's house who was already married. I, on the other hand, stayed in La Guaira for a year with Mamá. And from there we came to the U.S.

I arrived in New York on January 1st, 1955—another imported bee. I hovered over life in New York fairly calmly. It wasn't culture shock although I was not given the sample odors, like Mamá. It was all new to me. Yet I wasn't stung by the cacophony of smells or the noise of foreign foods, steel & body fluids. You see in Santo Domingo I was a schoolgirl. Lo tenía todo. Everything a young girl could want. And in New York I was also sheltered from the broken rhythm of shattered hopes. Upon our arrival in New York, Mamá already had an apartment lined up for us. She had some savings from selling Venezuelan honey dripping gold—or medallions of bee pollen to cushion the landing. So life as usual resumed. I went to a school where most of the girls were Puerto Rican. The most difficult part of life in New York was the cold weather. Soon after arriving in Manhattan, I contracted a skin disease centered around the stripes of my ribs. I was hospitalized for two days in Knickerbocker Hospital. The doctors said it was probably a result of the change in climate from oven to freezer. In these beehives other imported bees had to adopt new colors. Men rarely wore yellow guayaberas with black slacks. Although I believe they wore them below thick u.s.-made coats. Eventually the color shows. You can't hide a good linen guayabera.

The problem was that in New York the honey always had to be thawed.

```
I I        I I
O          O
I I        I I
O          O
```

"The work will be in the realm of the imagination as plain as the sky is to a fisherman—"
    —from *Spring And All,* William Carlos Williams

Omodé
tó iku—

murmured el negro viejo after his spirit mounted someone's head (Egungun). The spirit from another era, tiempo de la colonia, tiempo de *senseribó,* de los negros Kongo, negros Lukumí (Egungun). He said he knew the story—

Perhaps these were the last words he ever heard before the new pact was made. They said said it would be of utmost importance for him to observe the taboo of not blowing out candles. The candle would be the measure, the vehicle of communication between Iku & himself—blowing out the flicker would sever the dialogue. There would come a day when he would see (through mystical vision) a candle burning at someone's bedside. As an herbalist & diviner he could not heal that person. Iku would need that life; probably so that another one could be born somewhere else.

There was actually a time, maybe this is still going on, when a person's *ori inu,* (that is, literally the "head inside," the entity within that says "do this" or "do that" that says "follow this path" or "follow that"), would choose where & when it was going to be born, to whom, who would be the patron deity/orisha, what course his life would follow, and finally when will he breathe his last sigh. This of course would be contingent on what kind of destiny, what kind of head the ori inu chose—ori're or ori buruku, god or bad head. But then sometimes a head chooses to be born & to die soon after & born & die & continue this cycle—the head of an abiku.

There was actually a time, maybe this is still going on, when before burying the abiku, someone (El Niño's parents, priests presiding over his ritual) would clip a piece of ear from El Niño's corpse or cut half a pinky. The idea was to identify him as abiku when he returned. If he had such markings his history, the paths he's traversed, the heads he's petitioned, would be known. The proper amuletos can be prepared, the taboos observed. Somewhere along the lines though, the ori inu in conjunction his Orisha & Egun/ancestors must all make a pact with Iku.

El Niño actually wants to live.

The Pact:

1.
  The candle will be our medium for dialogue
  We must always
  be on speaking terms

2.
  When you see the candle by the bedside burning
  it will be my message to you:
  Do Not Touch!

3.
  You will heal through herbs &
  the words I give you to
  spray unto the solution

4.
  Never dress in black
  I may mistake you for
  someone ready to die

5.
  As much as possible
  do not speak wickedly or damn anyone

6.
  As much as possible
  stay away from funerals
  I like to work alone
  Death is death's work (Iku n'iku che)

7.
  Egun will be my messenger

8.
  You may also petition me
  through that white staff
  you know the one—
  with bells & snail shells
  You also know the chant

9.

Do not be tempted by possessions & titles
If you have patience
I will make possible
those you actually
will need

10.

Remember this pact
& I will give you health & long life (aiku)

All this was negotiated just prior to his birth. He probably kneeled before the Owner of the Sky while Iku, his patron Orisha, and many Egun sat watching with flywhisks in hand and full regalia (after all, one of their own was about to embark on his journey to the human world). The ilé aiyé.

He probably placed in circular fashion inside a big calabash all his choices, probably whispered into the gourd a slow "Ashé tó iba Eshu." We say probably because one thing is for sure, El Niño does not remember the details. In fact no one does (except the deities & Iku). No one remembers the details of their creation. No one remembers the destiny, the mission they chose, their personal Orisha, and most importantly the date of their last breath.

Memory & continuity. Keeping el hilo de la conversación. Never losing the wavy & fragile link that keeps you grounded to yr root. The dialogue with spirits that may tap yr left shoulder & all that. But no one remembers. No one remembers. Ésto si es trágico.

In order to recall the details of what went on in the other world, to map his destiny, El Niño must be taken for divination. And even then one session won't do it. The story will get revealed as his life turns each page & changes rhythm & the oracle is cast several more times. So they took El Niño to the diviner Edikán's house. After pouring libations & reciting the necessary ayuba prayers—greeting the creator, the ancestors, the divination, earth, wind, river, ocean, jungle, & crossroad orishas, Edikán cast the divining chain/ópele used by the babalawo. A picture began to emerge. He said the Orishas & Egun, collectively called ara orun or citizens of the other world, have given us certain verses & stories to deliver messages regarding the rhythms of our lives. He said El Niño's patron deity is Oshun but he will always have an affinity with Ogun & Obatalá. But most prominent is his close relationship with Egun, that is, the ancestors, Iku's messengers. He said it would be through a kinship with Egun that he would accomplish his most difficult tasks; even the arts of divination. He will be a mouthpiece for Egun.

Edikán said El Niño has a predisposition to a vivid imagination. Because of this there are & will be mysterious phenomena happening to him like visions & dreams of secret songs. He will not regard them as strange.

He said El Niño should be taught even at an early age the rigors of an herbalist. He should be taught at least how to recognize certain trees & plants, the healing properties of the most commonly used herbs, their harvesting times, how they mix & with what substances. All this will eventually lead to an encyclopedic knowledge not only of their healing properties but of their ability to alter the invisible rhythms that underlie most things.

Edikán said there will be certain resguardos that must be prepared so as to begin bridging the gap between Orishas, Iku, Egun, & himself. Even though El Niño's inner head/ori inu chose a good destiny in the other world, such destiny must be aligned with his physical head/ori in *this* world. It will be Orishas & Egun that will focus his life & help him fulfill the destiny he chose in the other world. He said beginning with the feet El Niño must be securely fastened to the earth so as to not depart too soon for the other world. (You see there is always the detail of Iku being overprotective. The relationship is like playing with a leopard—even an affectionate jab with its paw will cause a scar). The head will also have to be ritually prepared & fed with bits of white fruit among other ingredients & thus given a firm root, stability—"para que su cabeza no esté en el aire," he said.

We were witness to this event. We heard what needed to be done. There was actually a time, maybe this is still going on, when people consulted with the spirit world, the other world, on such occasions as the third month after birth. We collected the ingredients that would shape his destiny & began to assemble them. Much of them were from the river, the jungle, &

of course, the cemetery. We heard what needed to be done.

Ara Orun are hip to the images & subtle rhythms that stories & verses evoke. The same images & subtle rhythms running through our lives. Edikán said that barring some details of modernity, his life would follow a certain ancient story pertaining to the divination—

Ofun is like this/
Ofun ni jé bé—

The page continues to turn. The rhythm, the rhythm will come from dreams.

Herald of Cocos

Oye mira meng
listen hear—
do not be astonished
when you see a scorpion
cutting sugar cane . . .
it is the custom of my country
Don Masayá used to say
his voice full of rum
perched between mangos & chirimoyas
falling asleep on a hammock

A cosmic legacy begun
by three boats
Here big & beautiful negras
queens of wind & cemetery
provoke hurricanes
merely flapping their skirts
negras provoke(can) huracanes
flapping their skirts
Steel & iron clash
causing blooshed
causing steel & iron
to feast on blood

Don Masayá's memory drips the image
of that night
a black cape pis-
tol-whipped him & flew away
with his custom typewriter

with maracas on the keys—
an assassination attempt
on his rhythm
Don Masayá's memory drips
Don Masayá's memory drips the image
of many letters he received
already opened
of the echo of his parrot who perched
on his shoulder who sang divine danzón
the echo of his parrot's throat
slit.
Don Masayá's memory drips
Don Masayá's memory drips as he tumbles
off the hammock
startled by the touch of that colonel's
voice that colonel's
voice
tossing him to foreign soil

➥

A brief interruption
to listen to Miguelito Valdes's instruction
& Chano Pozo's percussion
to aid a cultural eruption

➥

The funeral is commencing
what shall we offer the healer of the sick:
17 lavender candles
a half-burned cigar

& a jar
of aguardiente
for tossing him to foreign soil
for tossing him to foreign soil

Do not be astonished
when revolution arrives on a cigar
wearing shokotó
& speaking in a trance—
Don Masayá used to say
his voice full of rum
waking from echoes of abuse
chanting his revenge:
the black cape
shall call me usted
typewriters shall taca-taca in maraca language
letters delivered by doves
macaws & african grays will perch on shoulders
& sing a son(g)
the colonel's voice
the colonel's voice shall be a ring of smoke
a memory of ashes—
tomorrow shall be the sweetest sugar cane

It was the roosters with
throat in full throttle
kee-keedee-croaking
in Spanglish . . .

it was the shores of Biscayne Bay
peppered with tar
with cans of Goya beans
with needles . . .
it was the belch
of criollo sauces
from mirrored cafeterias . . .
it was Calle Ocho singing
people screaming
with their hands . . .
it was Pepe, Carmen, Elena, Miguel
etcétera, etcétera...

it was why we shed our guayabera
& grew a tuxedo
shed our guayabera
& grew a tuxedo
We are of those who chose exile
from exiles

Yet now here we are
grand marshalls in a parade of roosters
buoying the polluted Biscayne
our Biscayne
eating enchilada de shrimp
screaming with our hands
looking for Pepe, Carmen, Elena
even Miguel
etcétera, etcétera...
The tuxedo didn't fit!!!
The tuxedo didn't fit!!!

Ceiba trees
palm trees
Cubano-Dominicano-Americano
& all that comes with it
We can see them/
those we can see our pearls
bouncing down 8th Street.
We can see pearls
surfing on ceiba trees
palm trees
mama we're coming home
Ceiba trees
palm trees
mamita we're coming home
mamita we're coming home

HERALD OF COCOS (I)

The breath of jesters
the tongues of queens
There are moments England
looses rhythm
& borrows legs from Africa
arms from Flamenco
a sonorous Taino echo
of canoa / canoe
There are moments in American midnights
this occurs on the Lower West Side
the Upper East Side
of the Atlantic

We summon from the sound of fruits
the aura of congas dripping a pulse
a display of cultural feathers
peacocks with ebony sheaths
ivory handles
ruby blades cutting
through chants of ignorance
We are a beyond generation
bereft of echoes
Antennas with eyes of rainbow
walking toward a point
just past the horizon
choosing the language we'll ignite
ready to fuel a generation of rainbows
arriving on plumed serpents

The heat & humidity licks
the comfort from our skin
Cities/barrios where la raza
is running
la raza escaping
the cold talcum powder falling
the sky is talking
dreams of migration
from tropical forestation
from islands vestid(o) green
to islands of electric(o) steel—
who is Cuba fleeing
where is Santo Domingo drifting
why is Puerto Rico sailing
Aqui is the steel that is frozen
Alla is the green that can't be forgotten

Through cities swimming in neon
crowds swaying like accordions
a tango of speech
many lips spell the message
in Lower East Side with pachangas
in Little Havana with guayaberas
in the Mission with Tolteca chancletas—
la raza has not melted
we are a beyond generation
walking toward a point
just past el horizonte

HERALD OF COCOS (II)

1.

Ko soro oda ni ofo
ko soro ofo ni oda
Osha re o
Adashé

2.

Un coco
un un
coco un
coco begins to speak
wiggling to the timba of timbero—
three drums for
three cocos for three islands
a throat for gods aboriginal
three drums si & yes
tres tambores—
okónkoló ki-lak ki-laking with itotelé
mama iyá ilú providing
bassy ba boom
        ba ba boom
              ra-ka-tak-boom
three drums speaking the language
of goatskins & echo
A straw mat encircled by seven sons & daughters
from Ifé
(first Yoruba city)
shaking quaking

seven symbols of sons & daughters:
red & white thunder
ivory wisdom
yellow & amber love
mother ocean
iron war
rainbow-colored wind
red & black herald

Ifa
master of the house of divination
secretary to the sky
ah-ah baba ashé Elegba
his mischievous doorman
will soon begin to speak
The sandy floor with teeth of straw mat
will become a mouth:

3.

Here we breed & love & survive
among the cold electric steel
the rusty concrete tattooed—
"Zorro 163" o "Jose 125"
"Juan 'n Carmen 110"
"Tito Loisaida"—
Aquí the cold has killed
the emerald from trees
alla the landscape is reaching
for the sky teaching
a generation of rainbows
can loose their color

Ko soro oda ni ofo
ko soro ofo ni oda
Osha re o
Adashé
We the people
whose history of skin
endowed us with an intense kiss
from the sun—
ko soro oda ni ofo
ko soro ofo ni oda
we the people
whose ancestors flew close to the sun
so says our Amerindian cheeks
our big African bembas
or 800 years of Moorish hair
waves so big you cd surf
the Spanish scalp—
we will not
cannot
sera suicide
gente santa
do not melt—

la raza moving
in blinks of migration
la raza dancing
with feet of realization
cósmica style
revolution style
arriving near a point
with wings like Icarus
Moctezuma's swords

Ogun's machete
& guaguancó bouncing off clouds

And the wings will not melt
& the swords will be sharper
the music clearer
as we arrive at a point
just past the horizon

THE CONNECTION BETWEEN
LAND & IDENTITY

You are of those whose machete
could mold a tropical rainbow
of those whose rainbow
could carve a tropical sun
sun that has witnessed
a tropical history

There were treasures at one point
fruit to feed a people
rattling y crashing in
the congestion of flora—
siguaraya, palo yaya, y jaguey
Giant tortoise with scars
on its back
famed for its thick blood
at times darting
a prophetic head
famed for looking real wise
rhythm real patient—
& yes también
the common rooster
strutting tribal rhythms of cool strength
the emerald world's muse

It is tattooed in oral tradition
every tree has mysteries
has stories
Mama Cachita said

decía Mama Cachita
hands stained with mango juice
the voice of delicate thunder
shattering any slyness
any mask
gawking roads may have
shaped

Tu/you
have arrived with hammock in hand
a river looks at you
with power
y you are then power
looking at a river
You are the smoke and mirrors
able to change the mute into sound
child of Hatuey
child of Mambí
bastard of Ferdinand

The cacophony of forced labor
dripping blood unto soil's memory
Ancestors clanking to the clave of machetes
cutting sugar cane
Mama Cachita's ancestors
tumbando caña con machete—
yr ancestors
yr name
was never writ
in snow was always writ
in sand
soothing yr feet

144

You are of those whose lineage
is stone & cowrie
sangre y monte
Tu eres de aquellos cuyos machetes
pudieran moldar un arcoiris
tropical
de aquellos cuyos arcoiris
pudieran armar un sol
tropical
sol que ha sido testigo
de una historia
tropical

Her hammock is hung between
fruits rattling crashing
in the congestion of flora
The Oshun River looking at her
with power
y Mama Cachita is power
seeing the Oshun
as she turns her back
bracelets jingling in full force
as she walks into an emerald world
once again
as you walk in her shadow
once again
yr back to that humid sun

Si de si o si de no
Some guayaberas spell nostalgia
some nostalgia spell guayaberas
Through the rhythmic kiss of spoon & tooth
the din of chandeliers
in mirrored cafeterias
air puffing rings of café
pastries on display in a museum of guayaba & cheese
Mongo conguero del Kongo
so says Santamaría
yes we can can
ruby'd Santa Barbara que es Shangó
golden lasso hanging from his neck
thunder rolling from caramelo hands
azucita marrón meaning
brown sugar—
listen for the wisdom of goatskins
yes we can can
yes we can can
as the sidewalks in Calle Ocho
move to the tumbao rumba of pedestrians

Aquí even the heat speaks Spanish
yes we can can
Guiro maraca & chekeré
hang as traffic lights
swinging like coconuts
to the gentle breeze saying hello then goodbye
then hello then goodbye

On the Art Deco sands of Miami Beach
the headlines read:
"Cuba Is On Vacation In Miami
Come Back Another Day"
yes we can can
But the gentry can not bear
the echo of today without
anecdotes of love left behind
of abuse
anecdotes of change
change the anecdotes
yes we can can

& drink tomorrow's café
without moving like a crab
yes we can can
as we wave to a wave
coming to save
a sleeve of nostalgia
yes we can can
but never
we can can never
wave to a wave
coming to save
a sleeve of forgotten chants

BILINGUAL BICULTURAL BY U.S.A.

Though my hair is not cocolo
Though my skin be olive
& when kissed by the sun
hue of copper
Though most my features thin
Though I have no accent
don't mistake for a second that I'm Caucasian
Yo soy de la raza brother!
Though I've listened to melting guitars through wah-wah pedals
I got the rumba timba
got the bomba plena merengue boom-boom
near my corazón
I got maracas swimming in my veins sister!
Though I've embraced the darlings of European lit
I carry my Pales Matos
Nicolás Guillén in my back pocket
Make no mistake
soy Cubano-Dominicano-Americano
That means I love my frijoles negros
my arroz con pollo, gandules
my platanos maduros shakes of fruta bomba
It means I got a protective brilliant mami
y un padre hermoso passionate
working hard building sculptures for people to live in
It means I lost my virginity with a girl named Maria Magdalena
Means I got at least one family member collecting food stamps
one family member too Catholic
at least one college educated
Means my parents were not allowed in a Maryland restaurant 1962

Means my father's uncle Puya is a santero
& I've seen breathing altars to Shangó, Oshun, y Yemayá
It means my nickname is Tito
It means my last name is Castro
y soy de la raza brother!
It means I speak la lengua while at home
& think in English the rest of the time
It means
I'm made in the U.S.A.
¿Comprendes?

IN THE BEGINNING (II)

There were wails echoing
from that side of the gulf
mining for hope
standing at the edge of sea
the desperate made everyone
quietly deaf
In the beginning there were chains
entwined on legs like serpents on sugar cane
chains spiraling out the earth
bleeding syrup made the steel stick
many a serpent's head was severed
There were processions of scars & snakebites
rattles talkin' 'bout the old country
drops of blood trickled from ankles
landed on this soil
(giving birth to a new people)

Crioooooollos!
Those with one foot strutting Cubano, Dominicano
Chicano, Boricua—
daughters de Caridad
abuelas de Altagracia
sons of Guadalupe named Lupito
tios & tias de Agueynaba

They gathered around the porch
& pitched poems from the narrative of their hymns
into the soothe of breeze
with maraca guitarra bongó

clave y conga—
who they be where
they come from
Regla, Matanzas, Luyano
Ázua, Aguas Buenas, y San Juan
They gathered around wooden porch
swaying on rocking chairs
rocking on hammocks
the wise the ancestral were remembered
Cups of memory spilled
to atone the present
refresh the future
Atone through tales of what came before—
Ñika La Liviana with white butterflies circling her hair
fish spawning at the feet of Bernarda
Miguel spilling poems that dangled on brass chain
all delivering messages que
todo tiene ashé
el café mango calabaza y maiz
have their consciousness
branches invading the sky
Un coco swaying to tún-tún of drum
waiting to crack open &
say something deep

Yet none of this was written in book
tale keeps changing
memory is survival
Tales in són in dance in poem
Tales of first arrivals
bereft of language
bereft of rest

Tales of the first job in la factoría
first home with certain hierbas
(herbs that alter the invisible)
Tales of initiations into the mysteries of rivers
thunder   spin of wind & ocean
serenity of clear light & gentle character/iwá pélé
Tales of drummings heard even in the homeland
(link 'tween memory & present)
So many stories within the backdrop
of imagination . . .

The wedding 'tween Afro y América
happened long before—
the sky was talking about migration
mix of peoples
you with kalalú
he con potato
she with viandas
we with potaje—
Dios with God con Olofin
Olofin/Dios/God
Santa Barbara con Shangó
Oshun y La Caridad del Cobre
Virgin de Regla y Yemayá
Obatalá con Las Mercedes
Ceramic faces often black
often wood
brown like betún
Drums still summoning heads of nature & spirit—

There is no god but in this ground
this monte we mow we tap

with machetes of sound y steel
this cotton reflecting the sun
thunder reaching for music
tambor y trueno
this wind that is both breeze y
hurakán
ocean that mothers those wrapped in big black rub-
ber doughnuts
rivers where we fish the tradition
of oracle y poesia

In the beginning
un coco tumbled & split
into four pieces
their pulp pointed skyward
todo está bien
the story continues . . .

Abakuá: Secret men's society in Cuba. Members are descendents of Calabar slaves.

Adagbó: (Yoruba) Good-bye.

Akara: (Yoruba) Traditional dish of mashed black-eyed beans.

Amalá: (Yoruba) Cornmeal porridge mixed with okra.

Araba: (Yoruba) Name of the ceiba tree.

Arará: (or Aradá) Descendants of slaves from Dahomey (now Benin).

Ashé olu batá: (Yoruba) Literally the power of the master drummer.

Babalawo: (Yoruba) Priest of Orunmila (orisha of knowledge and divination) who specializes in divination.

Batá: Ceremonial drums of Yoruba/Lukumí culture include okónkoló, itotelé, iya ilu.

Bomba: Also *Plena*. Traditional music from Puerto Rico.

Cascarilla: Spanish for lime chalk.

Carabalí: See Abakuá.

Ceiba: African Teak, or Silk-Cotton tree. Sacred tree in Yoruba culture.

Chekeré: see Shekeré.

Clave: Basic underlying rhythm in Latin and African music. Also a pair of sticks used to play the clave beat.

Danzón: Cuban musical form with elements of classical European music.

Ebioso: Dahomean vodun (god) of thunder and lightning. Similar to Shangó.

Ekué Abasî: God in the Abakuá pantheon.

Eko: (Yoruba) Cakes of cornmeal.

Elegba: Also Eleguá, Eshu. Messenger Orisha of the crossroads who is intermediary between man and orishas.

Eluaye ni mo se o; . . : (Yoruba) Chant to Obatalá meaning, "I am the carrier of the word, the carrier of the word is my father, Obatalá speaks speaks."

Ewé: (Yoruba) Herb, leaf.

Eyeife: (Yoruba) Favorable position in Lukumí system of coconut divination.

Eyibaríba eyibaríba nkamá . . : Chant to open Abakuá ceremonies.

Fila: (Yoruba) Traditional Yoruba hat.

Funfun: (Yoruba) White.

Ganga Nsasi: Principle deity in the Kongo pantheon in Cuba.

Guiro: Gourd or percussive musical instrument made from a gourd with ridges on a side which makes a scratching sound.

Hurakán: Taino Indian god of wind.

Iboru Iboya Iboshishé: (Yoruba) Greeting for a babalawo. Also "may the sacrifice be offered, may it be accepted, may it come to pass."

Ibu Aña: An avatar of Oshun with particular affinities with drums.

Idowu: (Yoruba) Name for a child born after twins.

Ifa: (Yoruba) Divination system presided by Orunmila.

Ifé: Birthground of the Yoruba. The "Yoruba Rome." Guini, Oyo, Dahomey, Takua, Iyesha are territories in West Africa and Yorubaland.

Iku: (Yoruba) The spirit embodied by death. Also death.

Ilé mo ku o . . . : (Yoruba) Chant greeting the earth and orisha or egun used in coconut divination.

Iré aiku shé alafia en: (Yoruba) Literally "a blessing of long life and peace."

Irúke: (Yoruba) Cow or horse-tail switch used as a symbol of authority in Yoruba culture.

Kere kere yan: (Yoruba) Chant praising twins meaning "little by little you become important."

Kimbombó: Okra as is called in Cuba.

Kongo: Also Congo. Name given in Cuba to the Bantu tribe and their descendents.

Ko soro oda ni ofo . . . : (Yoruba) Chant asking for truth not to be spoken as a lie or vice versa.

Ladekojú ibu yí odo . . . : (Yoruba) The river with the crown not worm-eaten.

Lukumí: Yoruba slaves and their descendants which heavily populated Cuba. Also the Yoruba spoken in Cuba which has elements of Spanish.

Malanga: Viand commonly eaten in the Spanish-speaking Caribbean.

Mariwó: (Yoruba) Dried palm fronds. Raffia.

Ñame: Yam or sweet potato.

Obatalá: Yoruba orisha of peace and purity; responsible for sculpting human beings.

Odu: (Yoruba) Verses from the Ifa and cowrie divination system.

Ogun: Yoruba orisha of iron, war, and creativity.

Oko Iyesha mo ilé mi . . . : (Yoruba) Chant meaning "I am a man from Iyesha, my mother's home is the river."

Oñi sokuta: (Yoruba) Sweet stone.

Otan iná: (Yoruba) Fiery or molten stone.

Orisha: (Yoruba) A god or goddess.

Osayin awa ni ye ti wi ti wi . . . :(Yoruba) From a chant telling Osayin (orisha of herbs and healing) that "we have survived."

Oshun: Yoruba female orisha of rivers, beauty, love, fertility, fine arts. Also a river in Nigeria.

Perejil: (Spanish) Parsley.

Rumba: Traditional Cuban musical form played usually with drums and other percussive instruments like claves, guiro, chekerés, etc.

Salakó: (Yoruba) A male born in a caul.

Shekeré: (Yoruba) A gourd with a net of beads used as a percussive instrument. In Spanish it is called chequere, or chekeré.

Sheketé: (Yoruba) Fermented corn liquor. Strong stuff.

Són: Cuban musical form; predecessor to salsa music.

Timba/Timbero: Cuban slang for the rhythm or swing of Latin music or drummer.

Tó Egungun: (Yoruba) "The ancestor has finished."

Yemayá: Yoruba female orisha of the ocean and symbol of motherhood.

Y'oko obi yoko bi . . . :(Yoruba) From a chant to Orunmila meaning "Sit down and study the kola nut" (divination).

Yoruba: Tribe in African west coast (now Nigeria) from which many slaves were captured and brought to the Caribbean. Major influence in Afro-Cuban culture. Their descendants were founders of santería or Regla de Ocha, the most predominant of Afro-Cuban religions which has very close similarities to traditional Yoruba religion and culture.